Solar System

KINGFISHER
LONDON & NEW YORK

First published as *Kingfisher Young Knowledge: Solar System* in 2006
Additional material produced for Kingfisher by Discovery Books Ltd.

Distributed in the U.S. by Macmillan, 175 Fifth Ave., New York, NY 10010
Distributed in Canada by H.B. Fenn and Company Ltd.,
34 Nixon Road, Bolton, Ontario L7E 1W2

Library of Congress Cataloging-in-Publication data has been applied for.

ISBN: 978-0-7534-6447-2

Kingfisher books are available for special promotions and premiums.
For details contact: Special Markets Department, Macmillan,
175 Fifth Avenue, New York, NY 10010.

For more information, please visit www.kingfisherbooks.com

Printed in China
1 3 5 7 9 8 6 4 2
1TR/0410/WKT/UNTD/140MA/C

Note to readers: the website addresses listed in this book are correct at
the time of going to print. However, due to the ever-changing nature
of the Internet, website addresses and content can change. Websites
can contain links that are unsuitable for children. The publisher cannot
be held responsible for changes in website addresses or content or
for information obtained through a third party. We strongly advise
that Internet searches be supervised by an adult.

Acknowledgments
The publishers would like to thank the following for permission to reproduce their material. Every care has been taken
to trace copyright holders. However, if there have been unintentional omissions or failure to trace copyright holders,
we apologize and will, if informed, endeavor to make corrections in any future edition.
b = bottom, *c* = center, *l* = left, *t* = top, *r* = right

Cover main Shutterstock/Stephen Girimont; cover *l* NASA; cover *r* NASA; 2–3 National Geographic; 4–5 NASA/Corbis; 6–7 NASA/SPL; 8*bl* Getty Images;
8–9 Getty Images; 10*cl* SPL; 10–11 NASA; 11*b* Corbis; 12–13 NASA/Corbis; 13*tl* Corbis; 13*bl* Mary Evans Picture Library; 16 Getty Images; 17*t* Getty
Images; 18–19 Corbis; 18*r* NASA; 19*t* Getty Images; 19*b* Getty Images; 20–21 NASA; 21*tr* NASA; 21*bl* NASA; 22*bl* Galaxy; 22*cr* NASA/SPL; 23*t* Corbis;
23*b* NASA; 24*c* SPL; 24–25 NASA; 25*b* Kobal Collection; 26–27*t* NASA/SPL; 27*cl* NASA/SPL; 27*br* Corbis; 28–29 Corbis; 30*c* SPL; 30–31 Corbis; 31*tr*
Corbis; 32–33 NASA/SPL; 33*tr* NASA/SPL; 37*br* NASA/SPL; 38*bl* The Art Archive; 38–39 Corbis; 39*br* Corbis; 40–41*t* Getty Images; 40–41*b* Galaxy Picture
Library; 42–43 NASA/Corbis; 47*br* Alamy Images; 48*r* Shutterstock Images/Vladmir Petrov; 48*b* Shutterstock Images/argonaut; 49*c* Shutterstock
Images/Giovanni Benintende; 49*b* Shutterstock Images/Sebastian Kaulitzhi; 52*t* Shutterstock Images/2Happy; 52*b* Shutterstock Images/Herb Sennet;
53*t* Shutterstock Images/Gheorghe Bunescu Bogdan Mircea; 53*l* Shutterstock Images/mashe; 56 Shutterstock Images/iofoto

Commissioned artwork on pages 34–35 and 40–44 by Daniel Shutt; commissioned photography on pages 44–47 by Andy Crawford.
Thank you to models Holly Hadaway and Sonnie Nash.

Solar System

Dr. Mike Goldsmith

KINGFISHER
NEW YORK

Contents

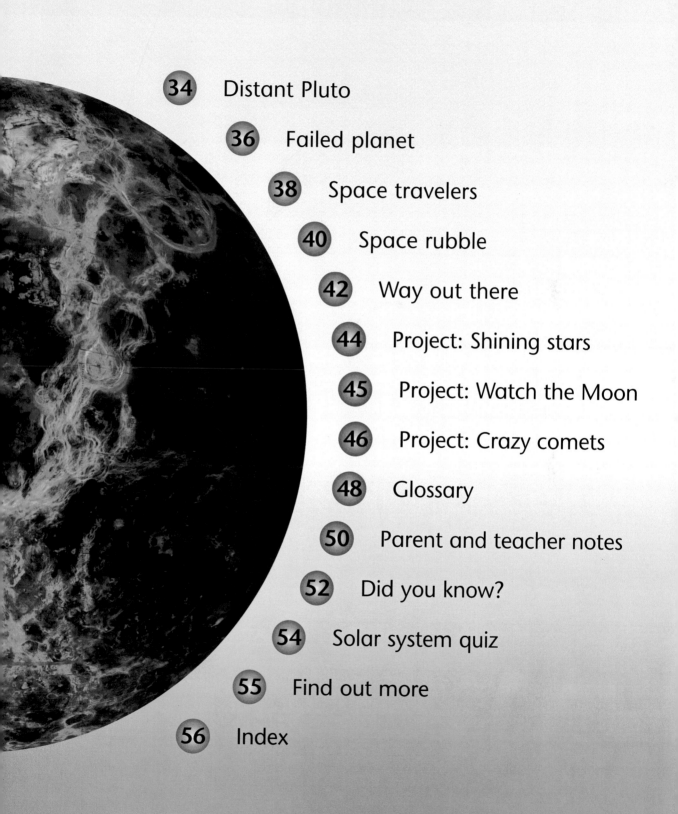

Solar system

Earth—the planet that we live on—the Sun, and the Moon are all parts of the solar system. It is called the solar system because everything goes around the Sun, and solar means "of the Sun."

Other worlds

There are eight planets in the solar system, and Earth is only one of them. Most of the planets also have moons going around them. Pluto used to be thought of as a planet. However, astronomers now call it a dwarf planet because it is so small.

Sun

Mars

Earth

Venus

Mercury

Pluto (dwarf planet)

Uranus

Neptune

Saturn

Jupiter

Space rocks

The Sun, planets, and moons are not the only things in the solar system. There are dwarf planets, asteroids, meteoroids, dust, and gases, too. Comets are like huge dirty snowballs. Asteroids are giant chunks of rock, and meteoroids are small pieces of rock.

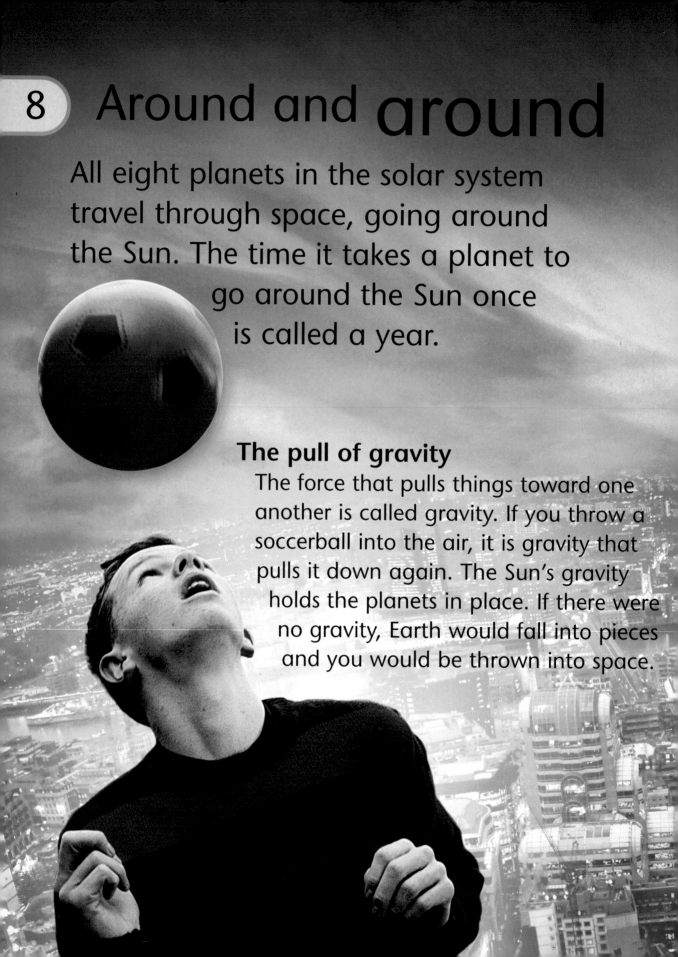

Around and around

All eight planets in the solar system travel through space, going around the Sun. The time it takes a planet to go around the Sun once is called a year.

The pull of gravity

The force that pulls things toward one another is called gravity. If you throw a soccerball into the air, it is gravity that pulls it down again. The Sun's gravity holds the planets in place. If there were no gravity, Earth would fall into pieces and you would be thrown into space.

Sun

Earth

Around the Sun

Earth goes around the Sun in about 365 days. Planets closer to the Sun have shorter orbits, so they go around it quicker. Mercury's year is 88 days.

Day and night

Each planet also spins around, causing it to have day and night. On other planets, day and night are not the same length as they are on Earth. The days on Venus are 243 times longer than ours!

Fiery star

The Sun is the only star in the solar system. It is so big that a million Earths could fit inside it! The Sun is also very hot—much hotter than an oven.

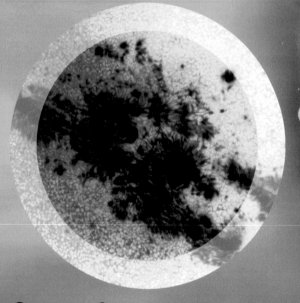

Spotty Sun
The surface of the Sun is always moving. Sometimes, dark, cool spots (above) form on the Sun's surface. These spots are called sunspots.

prominence

Great balls of fire

Prominences are giant masses of gas thrown off by the Sun. They look just like the leaping flames of a fire.

Warning! Hot Sun

It is dangerous to look directly at the Sun. When you play in the sunshine, always wear a hat, sunglasses, and sunscreen.

Fast Mercury

Mercury is a small planet that orbits very close to the Sun. The Sun's light makes Mercury's days very hot, but nights on Mercury are bitterly cold—much colder than any freezer. This is because there is no air to stop the heat from escaping.

Rocks galore!
The surface of Mercury is dry and rocky with gigantic cliffs. Mercury also has huge craters (hollows) caused by falling rocks millions of years ago.

Mighty *Mariner*

The spacecraft *Mariner 10* flew past Mercury three times in 1974 and 1975. It took photographs of about half of the planet.

God of speed

According to the myths of ancient Rome, Mercury was the messenger of the gods. He was supposed to fly quickly because he had wings on his heels.

Roasting Venus

Venus is the closest planet to Earth. On Venus, the sky is yellow and cloudy. The clouds trap the Sun's heat, making Venus a very, very hot planet.

Violent volcanoes

There are huge volcanoes on Venus. Some are much higher than any mountains on Earth. Venus's most famous volcano is called Maat Mons. It is more than 5.5 miles (9 kilometers) high. Sometimes on Venus, all of the volcanoes erupt at the same time, covering the whole planet in lava.

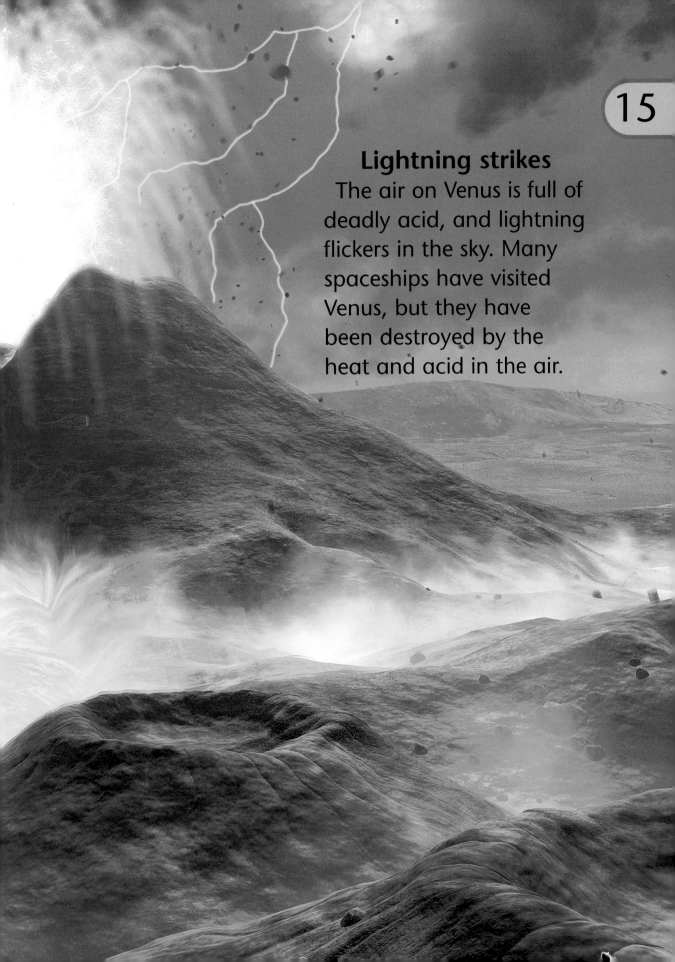

Lightning strikes

The air on Venus is full of deadly acid, and lightning flickers in the sky. Many spaceships have visited Venus, but they have been destroyed by the heat and acid in the air.

16) Our planet Earth

Earth is the planet that we live on. Most of its surface is covered with water, so from space, Earth looks blue. Together, the water, air, and warmth of the Sun make life on Earth possible.

Life on Earth

There are more than 30 million different types of plants and animals on Earth. They live everywhere, from the deepest ocean to the highest mountaintop.

dolphins

Restless planet

Compared to the other planets in the solar system, Earth has many volcanoes and earthquakes. Deep underground, Earth is so hot that the rock is molten. When a volcano erupts, the molten rock escapes onto the planet's surface.

Earth's Moon

The Moon is our closest neighbor in space. Just as Earth orbits the Sun, the Moon goes around planet Earth. There is no life or weather on the Moon—no clouds, wind, rain, or snow.

Hide-and-seek

The Moon takes about a month to go around Earth. It also takes a month to spin around. Because of this, we only ever see one side of the Moon from Earth. However, spaceships have traveled around the Moon, so we know what the far side looks like.

full Moon

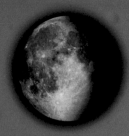
gibbous Moon

last quarter

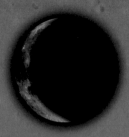
crescent Moon

Changing Moon

As the Moon moves, different parts of it are lit by the Sun. This makes it look as if the Moon is changing shape. The different shapes are called phases.

Crusty craters

Most of the Moon's craters were made millions of years ago when huge chunks of rock crashed into it.

Moon visit

The Moon is the only other world that people have visited. On the Moon, astronauts weigh one-sixth as much as they do on Earth.

Men on the Moon

In 1969, Neil Armstrong (born 1930) and Buzz Aldrin (born 1930) were the first astronauts to land on the Moon. They stayed there for 21 hours before returning to Earth.

Lunar Rover

In 1971, an electric car called the *Lunar Rover* was used to explore the Moon. So far, 12 people have visited the Moon. The last voyage was in 1972.

Famous footprints

Because there is no rain or wind to disturb the dust on the Moon's surface, the footprints left by the astronauts in 1969 are still there.

Rusty Mars

Mars is red because it is rusty. There is a lot of iron in the soil, and the air on Mars has made it turn red— just like a rusty nail on Earth.

Poles of ice

Like Earth, the poles (the top and bottom ends of the planet) of Mars are covered in ice. The ice becomes thicker in the winter.

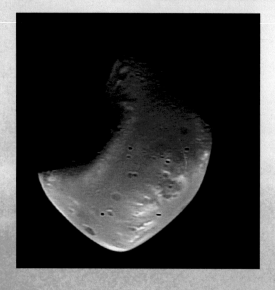

Two moons

Mars has two tiny moons called Phobos (left) and Deimos (above). Phobos is moving closer and closer to Mars, and scientists think that one day it will crash into Mars.

Mighty Mons

Mars's surface is covered with deserts, canyons, craters, and gigantic dead volcanoes. Olympus Mons is the tallest volcano in the solar system. It is 15 miles (24 kilometers) high.

Living with Martians

Long ago, the air on Mars was thicker, and there were valleys filled with water. This means that there may have been life on the red planet.

Super *Spirit*

In 2004, *Spirit* landed on Mars after a seven-month trip through space. It sent pictures of Mars back to Earth and studied the soil and rocks there.

Strange soil

In 1976, two robot probes called *Viking I* and *Viking II* landed on Mars to look for life in the soil. The soil behaved in a strange way—but this is probably because it contained unfamiliar chemicals, not living things.

Martian monsters

Until recently, people thought there might be humanlike creatures on Mars. We now know this is not true, but filmmakers often show Martians as strange green men.

Giant Jupiter

Jupiter is the biggest planet. It is 1,300 times the size of Earth. It spins around quickly, so its days are only ten hours long. Because it does not have a solid surface, it is impossible to land a spaceship on Jupiter.

Great Red Spot
Jupiter is a very stormy planet. One storm has already lasted for more than 300 years! From Earth, this storm looks like a giant red spot.

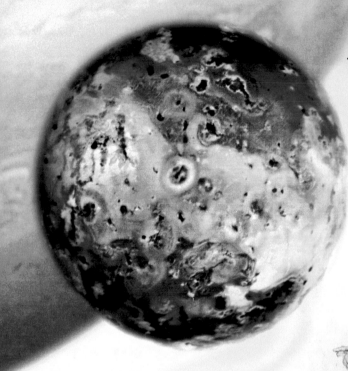

Marvelous moons

Jupiter has many moons. The moon shown here, Io, has active volcanoes. Europa has an icy surface, and Ganymede is the biggest moon in the solar system—it is even bigger than the planet Mercury.

Great Galileo

In 1609, using a homemade telescope, the Italian scientist Galileo Galilei (1564–1642) discovered four of Jupiter's moons.

Ringed Saturn

Many people think that
Saturn is the most beautiful
planet in the solar system. Saturn
is so light that if there were an ocean
big enough, the planet could float in it.

Rings of rock

Saturn's rings are made up of billions
of pieces of rocks and dust. Although
the planets Jupiter, Uranus, and
Neptune also have ring
systems, theirs are not
as bright or as big
as Saturn's.

Studying Saturn

The *Cassini* probe was launched in 1997 on a mission to study Saturn, its rings, and its moons. *Cassini* arrived in 2004.

Cold Uranus

Uranus is a huge, cold, blue-green world far out in space. It is surrounded by many black rings and icy moons. Because of the strange way it spins, nights on some parts of Uranus can last for more than 40 years.

Twisted Miranda

The surface of Miranda, one of Uranus's moons, is very uneven. It has cliffs over 12 miles (20 kilometers) high and enormous ridges, grooves, and craters.

Uranus

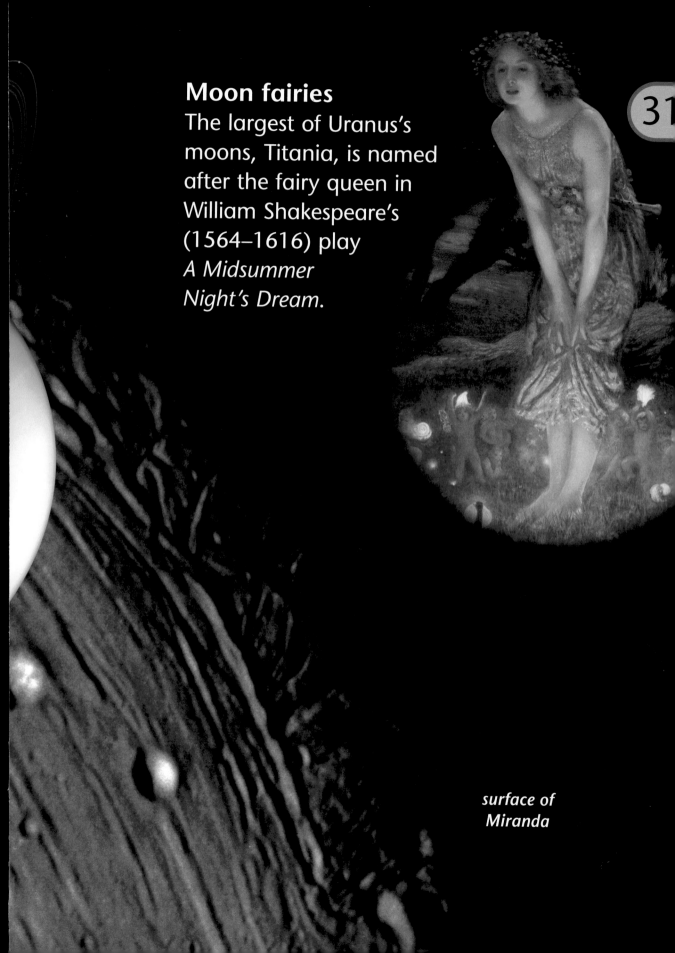

Moon fairies

The largest of Uranus's moons, Titania, is named after the fairy queen in William Shakespeare's (1564–1616) play *A Midsummer Night's Dream.*

surface of Miranda

Stormy Neptune

Neptune is an extremely cold, blue world. It is so far away from Earth that the space probe *Voyager 2* took 12 years to reach it!

Cold volcanoes

This picture shows the surface of Triton, one of Neptune's moons. Triton has huge volcanic eruptions of liquid nitrogen.

Stormy clouds

Neptune is the stormiest planet. The winds there can blow up to 1,200 miles per hour (2,000 kilometers per hour)—three times as fast as Earth's hurricanes! Sometimes, storm clouds appear as white streaks or dark spots on its cloudy surface.

Distant Pluto

Pluto is called a "dwarf planet" because it is so small. It is farther from the Sun than the main planets. It is tiny, reddish brown, and smaller than Earth's Moon.

Sun

Charon

Colossal Charon

Pluto is so small that it
can be seen from Earth
only with a powerful
telescope. It has a moon
called Charon. Charon
was only discovered in
1978. It is darker and
grayer than Pluto, but
like Pluto, it is also
covered in rocks and ice.

In the dark

If you visited Pluto, the Sun
would look like a bright star.
Pluto is so far away from the
Sun that it is always dark there.
No spaceship has reached this
dwarf planet, so we do not
know what it really looks like.

Failed planet

Beyond Mars and Jupiter there are billions of pieces of rock and metal called asteroids. They are much smaller than planets. Scientists believe that the asteroids are pieces of a planet that failed to form.

Asteroid belt

Most asteroids can be found in two regions, or "belts." One of the belts is between Mars and Jupiter, and the other is beyond Neptune.

Asteroid Ida

Ida is a small, potato-shaped asteroid with its own tiny moon. In 1993, the *Galileo* space probe took pictures of Ida as it flew past.

Space travelers

Comets are visitors from the outer parts of the solar system. They are lumps of ice and dust—a little like dirty icebergs drifting through space. When the comets come close to the Sun, the ice turns to gas.

Return of the comet

All comets orbit the Sun. Some take hundreds, thousands, or even millions of years to return. Halley's comet returns only every 76 years. This famous tapestry shows Halley's comet (top left) in A.D. 1066.

Two-tailed Hale-Bopp

As a comet moves closer to the Sun, it forms two tails. One of the tails is made of gas and the other of dust. The gas tail points away from the Sun. In this picture of comet Hale-Bopp, the gas tail is blue and the dust tail is whitish.

Comet crash!

In 1994, pieces of a comet called Shoemaker-Levy 9 broke apart and crashed into Jupiter. This left patches in Jupiter's atmosphere that lasted for many months.

Space rubble

There are many pieces of rock and dust drifting through space. These objects are called meteoroids. Many meteoroids are left behind by comets.

Shooting stars!

Every year, 200,000 tons of meteoroids fall through Earth's atmosphere. As large meteoroids rush through the air, they become so hot that they glow. This falling glow is called a meteor, or shooting star.

Huge Hoba

Meteors that land on Earth are called meteorites. The heaviest known meteorite is Hoba West. It was found in 1920 in Namibia and weighs around 66 tons—that is about as heavy as nine elephants!

Way out there

In 1961, a Russian named Yuri Gagarin (1934–1968) became the first person to travel into space and go right around Earth. Since then, many astronauts have traveled through space.

Drifting through space

Exploring space is dangerous. Sometimes, astronauts leave their spaceships to "walk" in space. This astronaut is wearing a device that can push him back to his spaceship if he starts to drift away.

Life in space

In space there is no air, nothing has any weight, and there is no "up" or "down"—which can make life difficult. Some space travelers get spacesick, just like people on Earth get seasick.

Shining stars

Bedroom planetarium

Dome-shaped buildings called planetariums have lights that show the night sky. Use a flashlight to make your own star in the sky.

You will need:
- Flashlight
- Pencil
- Black poster board and white paper
- Scissors
- Tape

1 Place the flashlight on the poster board so that you can trace around the front end of it. Using a pencil, trace carefully around the flashlight.

2 To make a star-shaped stencil, draw a star on a piece of paper and cut it out. Place the stencil inside the flashlight shape and trace around it.

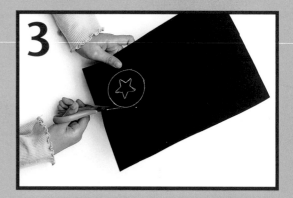

3 Using the scissors, carefully cut out both shapes. You should now be left with a circle of poster board that has a star shape in the middle.

4

Use tape to attach the poster board to the front of the flashlight. Turn off all the lights in the room and shine the flashlight on the ceiling to see your star. For something different, try cutting out a shape of the Moon.

Watch the Moon

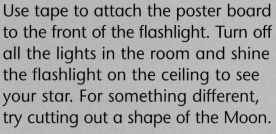

Find the craters!

Not only are there craters on the surface of the Moon, but every month, our closest neighbor also appears to change shape. On a clear night, use binoculars to look for the Moon's craters. Never look at the Sun with binoculars because this will damage your eyes.

Whenever you see the Moon—whether at night or during the day—draw its shape on the correct date on a calendar. After a few months, your calendar will show you how the Moon seems to go through a series of changes (called phases).

Crazy comets

Finding new comets
New comets are discovered every year, but most of them are too faint to see without using binoculars or a telescope.

1

To make big pieces of space dust, place two cookies on a plate. Using the wooden spoon, crush the cookies into large pieces.

You will need:
- 2 large plates
- Cookies
- Wooden spoon
- Teaspoon
- Colored sprinkles
- Chocolate sprinkles
- Ice-cream scoop
- Chocolate ice cream
- Ice-cream cone

2

To make smaller pieces of space dust, add a large handful of colored sprinkles to the crushed cookies.

3

For extra space dust, add two handfuls of chocolate sprinkles to the mixture. Mix the space dust using a teaspoon.

For the comet's head, use an ice-cream scoop to make a ball of ice cream. Cover the ball of ice cream in the dust mixture.

To make the comet's tail, carefully place the ice-cream ball onto an ice-cream cone. Push down lightly on top of the ball to secure it.

Roll the ice cream back into a ball shape. If the ice cream has started to melt, put it on another plate in the freezer.

Although you would never be able to eat a real comet, such as Hale-Bopp, this one is made from delicious ice cream, so it tastes great!

Glossary

asteroid—a chunk of rock that circles the Sun between the orbits of Jupiter and Mars

astronaut—someone who travels into space

astronomer—a scientist who studies the stars and space

atmosphere—a mixture of gases that surrounds a planet

cliff—a steep, high edge of land

comet—an object that is made from ice, rocks, and gas with a shining tail. It orbits the Sun like a planet.

crater—a wide hole caused by something crashing into the ground or by volcanic activity

desert—a very dry area of land where hardly anything grows

earthquake—an earth movement that causes the ground to shake and crack

erupt—when a volcano erupts, it throws out hot lava and ash

force—a pushing or pulling action that alters the movement or shape of an object

gravity—the force that pulls objects such as the Sun, planets, or moons toward one another

meteorite—the remaining part of a meteoroid that falls to Earth

meteoroid—a piece of rock that travels through space and burns brightly when it enters Earth's atmosphere

Moon—the object that moves around Earth, seen as a bright circle or crescent in the night sky. Some other planets have moons.

myth—a made-up story

orbit—the path of one object around another object in space

planet—an enormous spherical object that orbits a star. For example, Earth orbits the Sun.

ridge—a long, narrow piece of high land

rusty—describes the red color caused by iron reacting with air and water

sunspot—a dark, irregular patch on the surface of the Sun

tapestry—artwork embroidered on a piece of heavy cloth

volcano—a mountain with openings at the top where lava and gas escape

voyage—a long journey

The content of this book will be particularly useful in helping to teach and reinforce concepts and skills in science and language arts curricula. It also provides opportunities for crosscurricular lessons in art, history, and math.

Extension activities

Language arts
Writing
1) If you could explore any planet, which one would you choose? Imagine your expedition and write a journal describing your discoveries, adventures, and challenges.

2) Each planet is featured in a two-page spread giving basic information. Pick one planet and research to find out more about it. Write and illustrate a one-page report. If possible, give your report in class.

Speaking and Listening
The silly sentence "My Very Enthusiastic Mother Just Served Us Noodles" is a way to remember the names of all eight planets in order. Each word begins with the same letter as one of the planets. Make up some more sentences and share them with your friends and classmates.

Science
The topic of the solar system relates to the scientific themes of locations (pp. 6–7, 12–19, 22–23, 26–27, 30–39); movement (pp. 6–7, 12–13, 18–19, 26–27, 30–33, 38–41); and properties of objects in the sky (pp. 6–7, 10–19, 22–23, 26–41). Additional themes include cycles and seasons (pp. 8–9, 18–19, 30–31, 38–39); forces and motion (pp. 8–9, 18–19, 32–33); geologic features (pp. 12–19, 22–23, 26–41); and space exploration (pp. 12–15, 18–21, 24–25, 26–29, 32–37, 42–43).

Crosscurricular links
1) *Literature and history:* Most planets and many of their moons were named after people in Greek and Roman mythology (p. 13). Some (p. 31) were named after well-known figures in other literature. List the names of the planets and moons mentioned in

this book and research to find out where their names came from. Extra challenge: There are many more moons! Scientists continue to discover—and name—others in addition to those mentioned here.

2) Art: Each of the articles in this book gives information about the colors of the different planets. Draw and illustrate a lineup of all eight planets, showing as many details as possible. Take a look at *www.nasa.gov* for some spectacular images.

3) Science and math: A scale model can help us comprehend the incredible vastness of our solar system. For example, if Earth were the size of a peppercorn, Jupiter would be about the size of a chestnut. Scale models can also help us compare the distances between planets: if Earth were 3 feet (1 meter) from the Sun, Jupiter would be about 15 feet (4.5 meters) away. Ask an adult to help you search the Internet for "scale model of solar system" to find a model that you can measure out to show the comparative sizes of the planets, the distances between the planets, or both.

Using the projects
Children can do these projects at home. Here are some ideas for extending them:

Pages 44–45: A constellation is a group of stars in a pattern thought to resemble an animal, object, or mythological figure. Use reference materials to find some examples. Copy or trace a constellation pattern and glue it to a sheet of black paper. Put the paper on a soft surface such as thick cardboard or the carpet and carefully poke a hole through each dot with a pushpin. Hold the paper up to the light to see your constellation.

Page 45: Look for patterns as you record a complete cycle of the Moon's phases. Use the patterns to predict the shape of the Moon on the nights when clouds keep you from actually seeing it.

Did you know?

- Despite being the closest planet to the Sun, Mercury is not the warmest. Venus is warmer. Mercury is one of the coldest planets in the solar system. This is because it has no atmosphere to trap heat.

- Asteroids that cross the orbit of Earth as they move around the Sun are called Apollo asteroids. Scientists believe that an Apollo asteroid could have hit Earth about 65 million years ago, causing the dinosaurs to become extinct.

- Some people believe that astronauts may someday travel to and live on Mars. Mars is more like Earth than any other planet: it has volcanoes, polar icecaps, climatic seasons, and clouds.

- Meteorites have been known to kill livestock and damage houses and cars.

- The same side of the Moon always faces Earth. This means that we never see the other side.

- The pressure is so great on Jupiter that anything entering its atmosphere would be immediately crushed, including a spacecraft.

- One year on Jupiter is equal to 12 years on Earth.

- Neptune is the fourth-largest planet in the solar system. Sixty Earths could fit inside it.

- Jupiter is so massive that if it were hollow, all of the other planets could fit inside it.

- When Earth enters a meteoroid stream left by a comet, a meteor shower is produced. These showers can be predicted and come every year or so. Meteor showers can be spectacular, involving more than 100 meteors per hour.

- Violent storms occur on Saturn, some with winds up to 1,100 miles per hour (1,770 kilometers per hour)!

- Early astronomers believed that the dark patches on the surface of the Moon were oceans.

- Astronauts need to be tied to their beds when they are asleep in space so that they do not float away.

- Without the Sun, life on Earth would not exist. It would be so cold that no living thing would be able to survive, and our planet would be completely frozen.

- Uranus is about four times as large as Earth and 15 times as heavy.

- Mars has seasons similar to our planet, but they last much longer. For example, summer on Mars lasts 199 Earth days.

- Without a spacesuit, an astronaut's blood would boil in space!

- It takes Uranus 84 years to make one orbit of the Sun. It would always be your birthday on Uranus—there is only a single day and night every year.

- Venus spins "backward," so the Sun rises in the west and sets in the east.

- Venus is the brightest planet in Earth's night sky. Only the Moon (which is not a planet) is brighter. Venus outshines the other planets because its thick clouds reflect the Sun's light.

- In space, astronauts are up to 2 inches (5 centimeters) taller than they are on Earth. There is less gravity pushing down on their backbone in space, so it stretches. As soon as the astronauts return to Earth, their height goes back down to what it was before.

Solar system quiz

The answers to these questions can all be found by looking back through the book. See how many you get right. You can check your answers on page 56.

1) How many days does it take for Earth to go around the Sun?
A—365
B—12
C—1

2) Nights on Mercury are . . .
A—extremely hot
B—bitterly cold
C—stormy

3) Water, warmth from the Sun, and what else is needed to make life on Earth possible?
A—acid
B—volcanoes
C—air

4) What is Earth's closest neighbor in space?
A—Venus
B—the Moon
C—Jupiter

5) What color is Mars?
A—blue
B—green
C—red

6) Jupiter is very . . .
A—hot
B—small
C—stormy

7) What is Uranus's largest moon called?
A—Titania
B—Tracy
C—Titanic

8) How many different types of plants and animals are there on Earth?
A—more than 30 million
B—more than 20 million
C—more than ten million

9) Halley's comet returns once every . . .
A—100 years
B—45 years
C—76 years

10) What is a meteorite?
A—a meteor that lands on Earth
B—a meteor that lands on the Moon
C—a meteor that breaks up in space

11) Which planet is the stormiest?
A—Earth
B—Uranus
C—Neptune

12) An asteroid is . . .
A—a failed planet
B—a failed star
C—another Sun

Find out more

Books to read

Exploring the Solar System by John Farndon, Raintree, 2010

Navigators: Stars and Planets by Dr. Mike Goldsmith, Kingfisher, 2008

Space! Our Solar System and Beyond by Peter Riley, Franklin Watts, 2008

Beyond: A Solar System Voyage by Michael Benson, Abrams Books, 2009

Solar System by Emily Bone, Usborne, 2010

Places to visit

Denver Museum of Nature and Science
www.dmns.org/planetarium/current-shows/cosmic-journey
Cosmic Journey, a short movie at the museum's planetarium, lets you travel through the solar system at many times the speed of light, observing the planets and their moons close-up.

Kennedy Space Center
www.kennedyspacecenter.com
Visit NASA's launch headquarters, where you can tour launch areas, see rockets, test out spaceflight simulators, and even view a launch. The museum offers guided tours and special programs, including the opportunity to have lunch with an astronaut.

Smithsonian National Air and Space Museum
www.nasm.si.edu
View exhibitions about the history of human space travel, including missions to the Moon, and learn about the future of space exploration. The museum displays many space-related artifacts donated by NASA, and you can see the retired space shuttle *Enterprise* at the museum's Steven F. Udvar-Hazy Center.

Websites

www.kidsastronomy.com
Learn about the solar system, the planets, and moons with facts, diagrams, and interesting animations.

www.nationalgeographic.com/kids
Find out how the solar system began, with facts and videos. You can test your knowledge afterward with a fun quiz.

www.nasa.gov/audience/forkids/kidsclub/flash/index.html
At the NASA Kids' Club website, play lots of games involving space and the solar system.

http://spaceplace.nasa.gov/en/kids/
Find fun projects and games, plus watch animations and read interesting facts about our solar system on NASA's Space Place website.

Solar system quiz answers

1) A	7) A
2) B	8) A
3) C	9) C
4) B	10) A
5) C	11) C
6) C	12) A